My Family Keeps Fit

David Tunkin

My family is active.
We like to keep fit.

3

My mom likes to walk.
She walks to work.
Walking helps keep her fit.

My **dad** likes to jog.
He jogs around the park.
Jogging helps keep him fit.

My **brother** likes to shoot baskets. He shoots baskets at the park. Shooting baskets helps keep him fit.

DO NOT
HOLD ONTO RING

My **sister** likes to swim.
She swims at the swimming pool.
Swimming helps keep her fit.

I like to ride my bike.
I ride my bike on the bike path.
Riding my bike helps keep me fit.
How do you keep fit?